Fuck Off

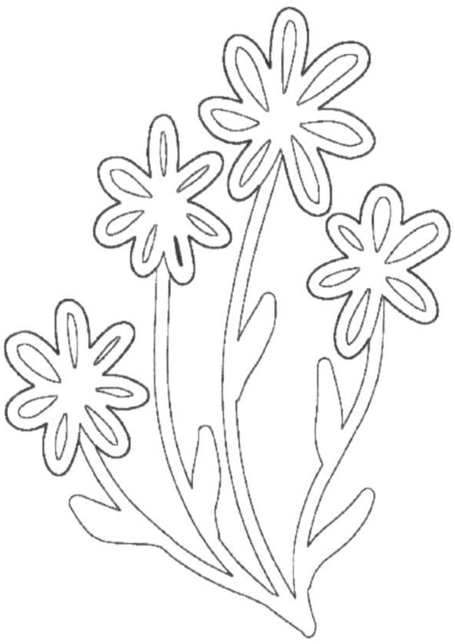

THE SWEAR WORD COLORING BOOK FOR ADULT.

ENJOY COLORING!!!

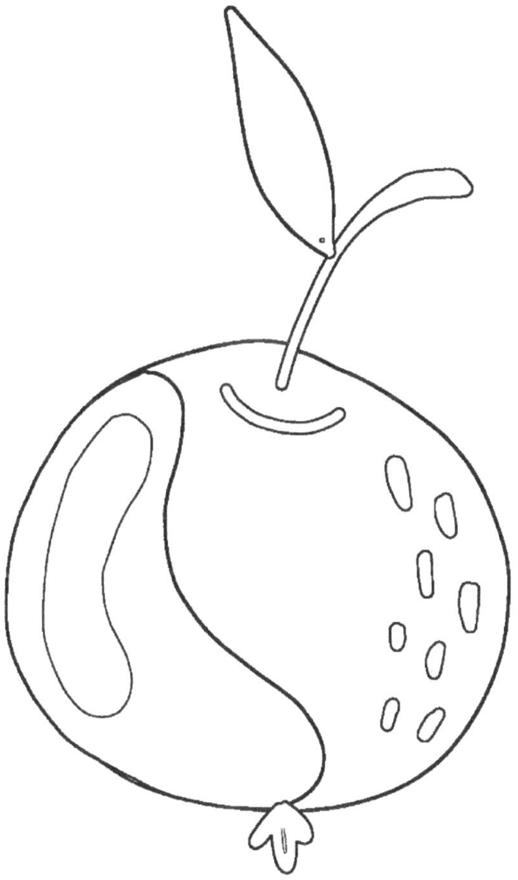

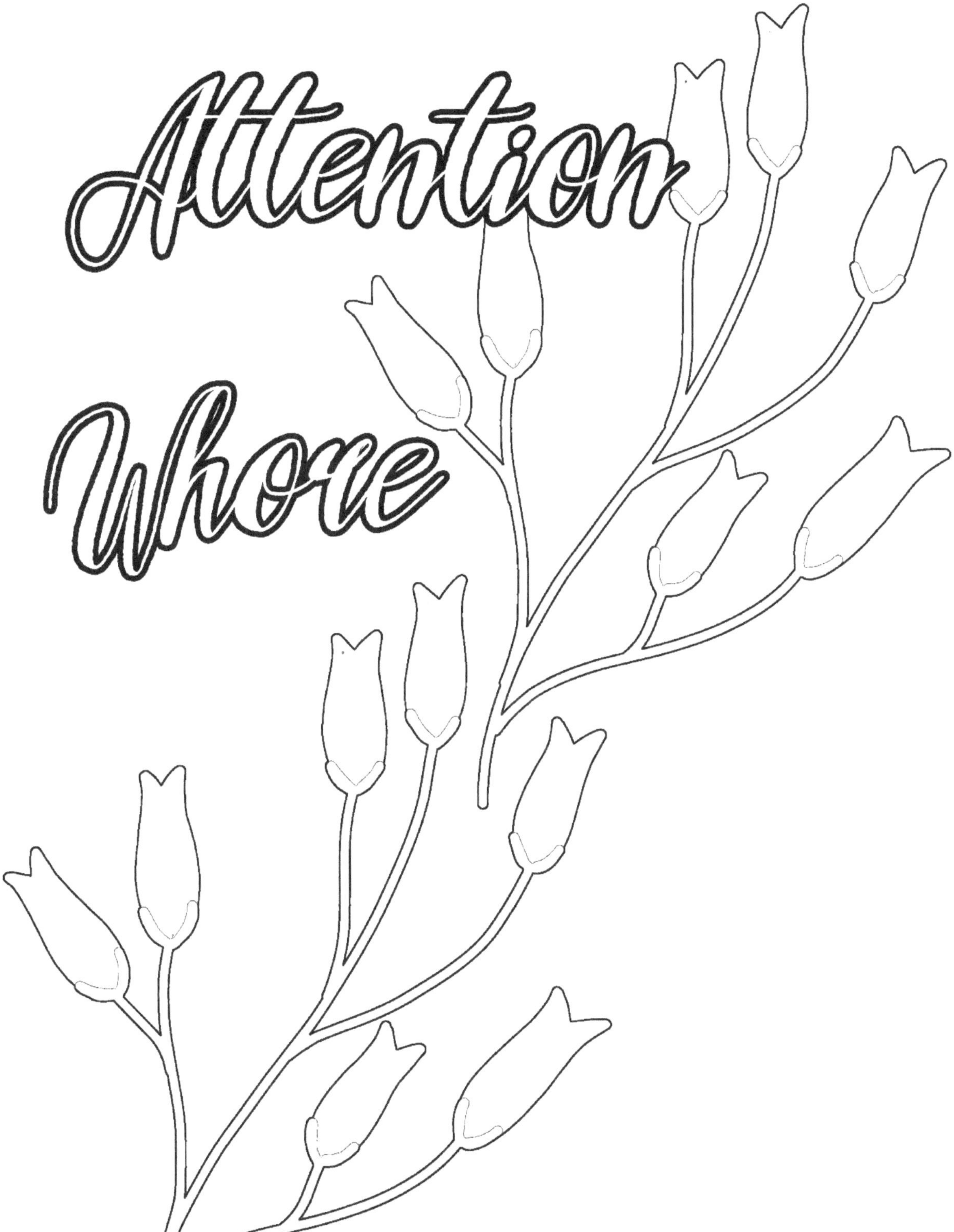
Attention
Whore

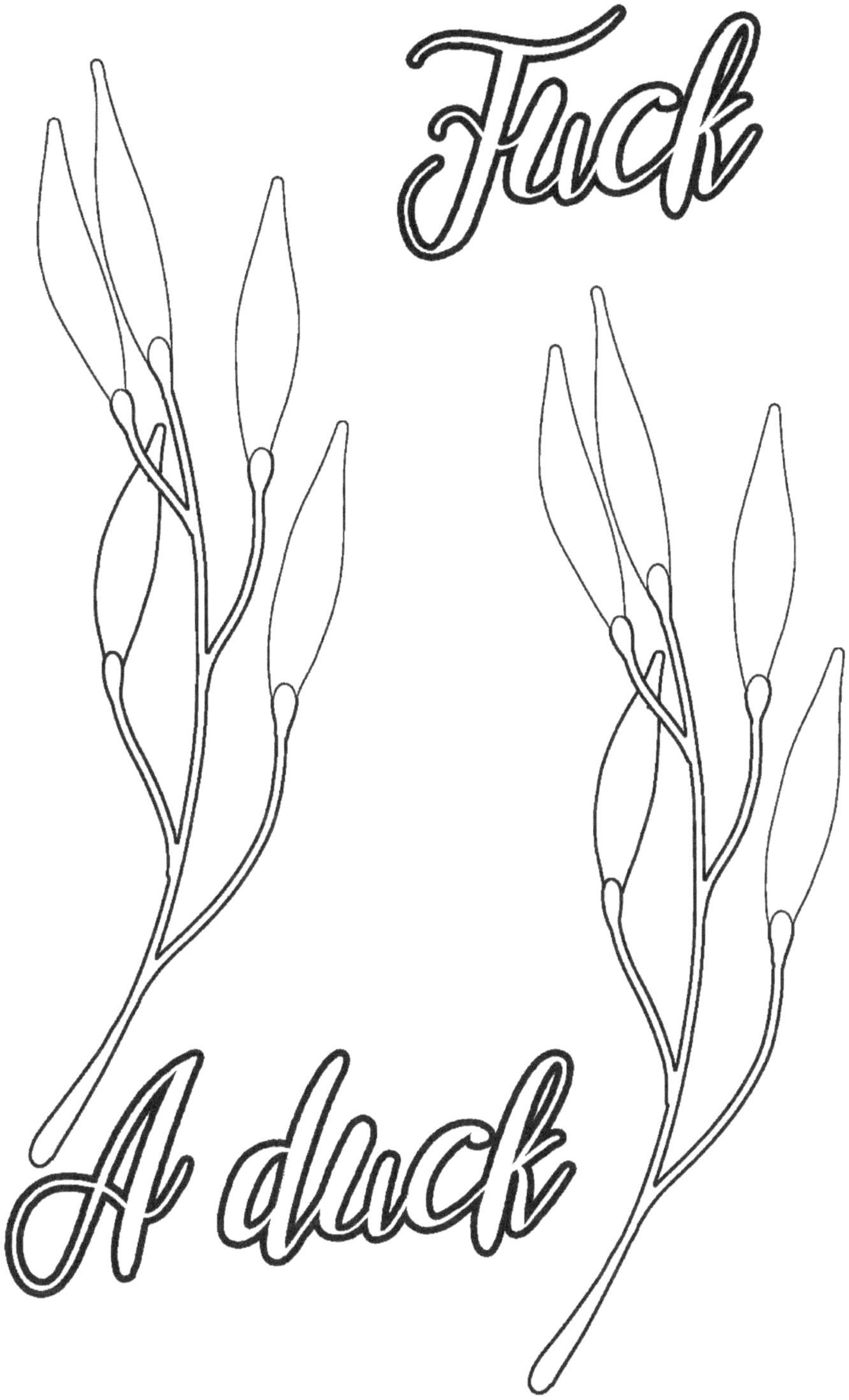
Fuck
A duck

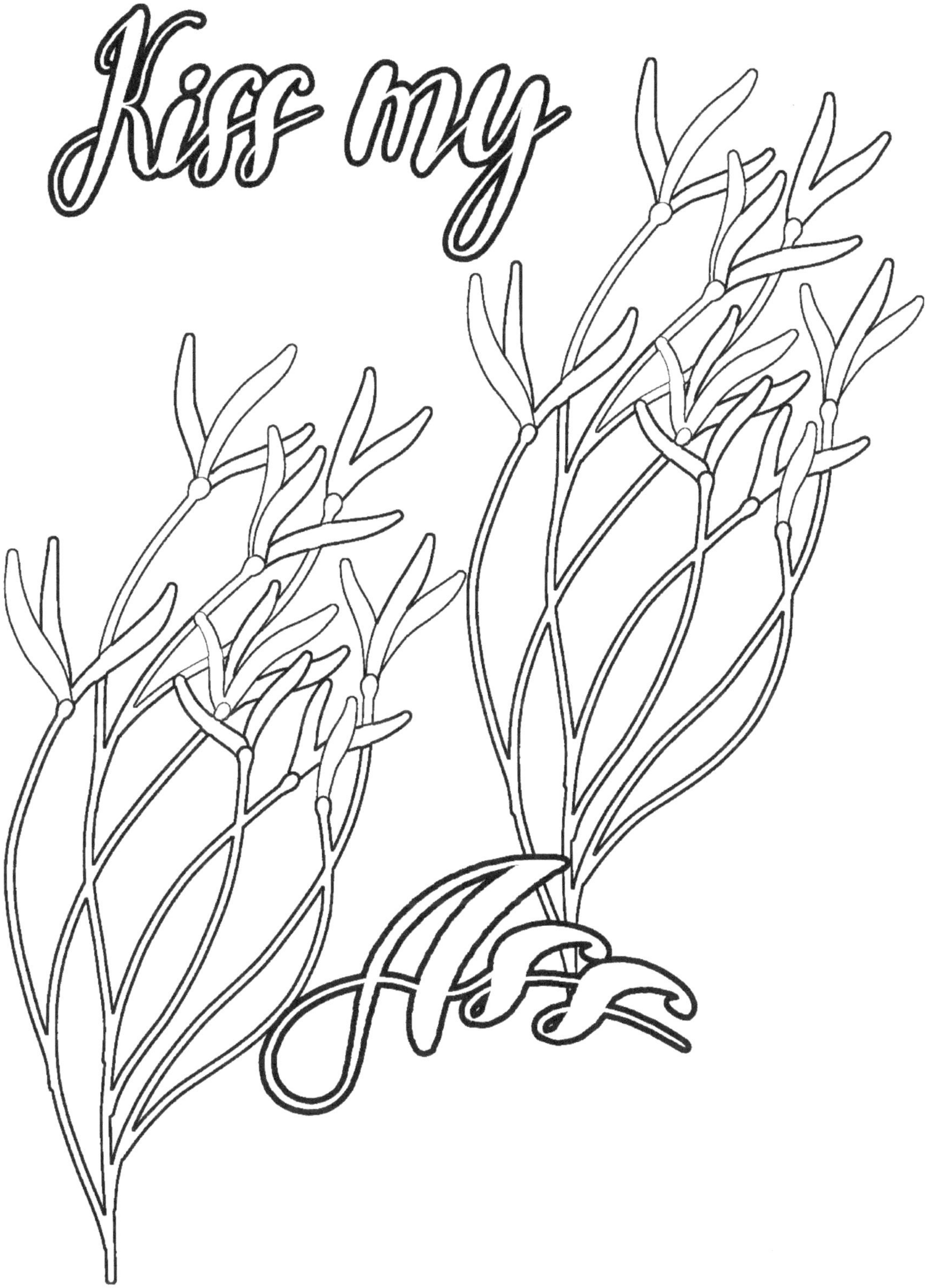
Kiss my
Ass

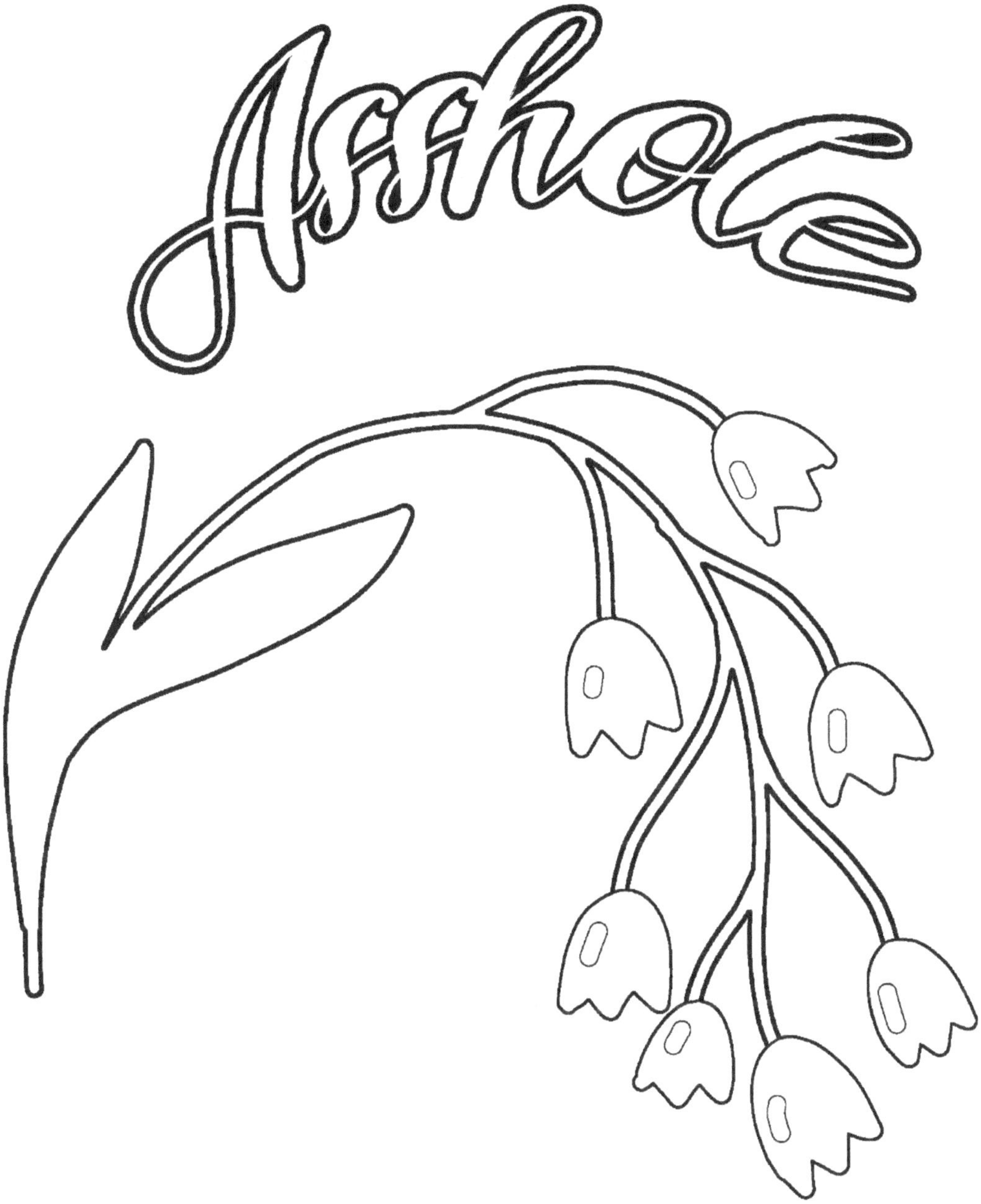
Asshole

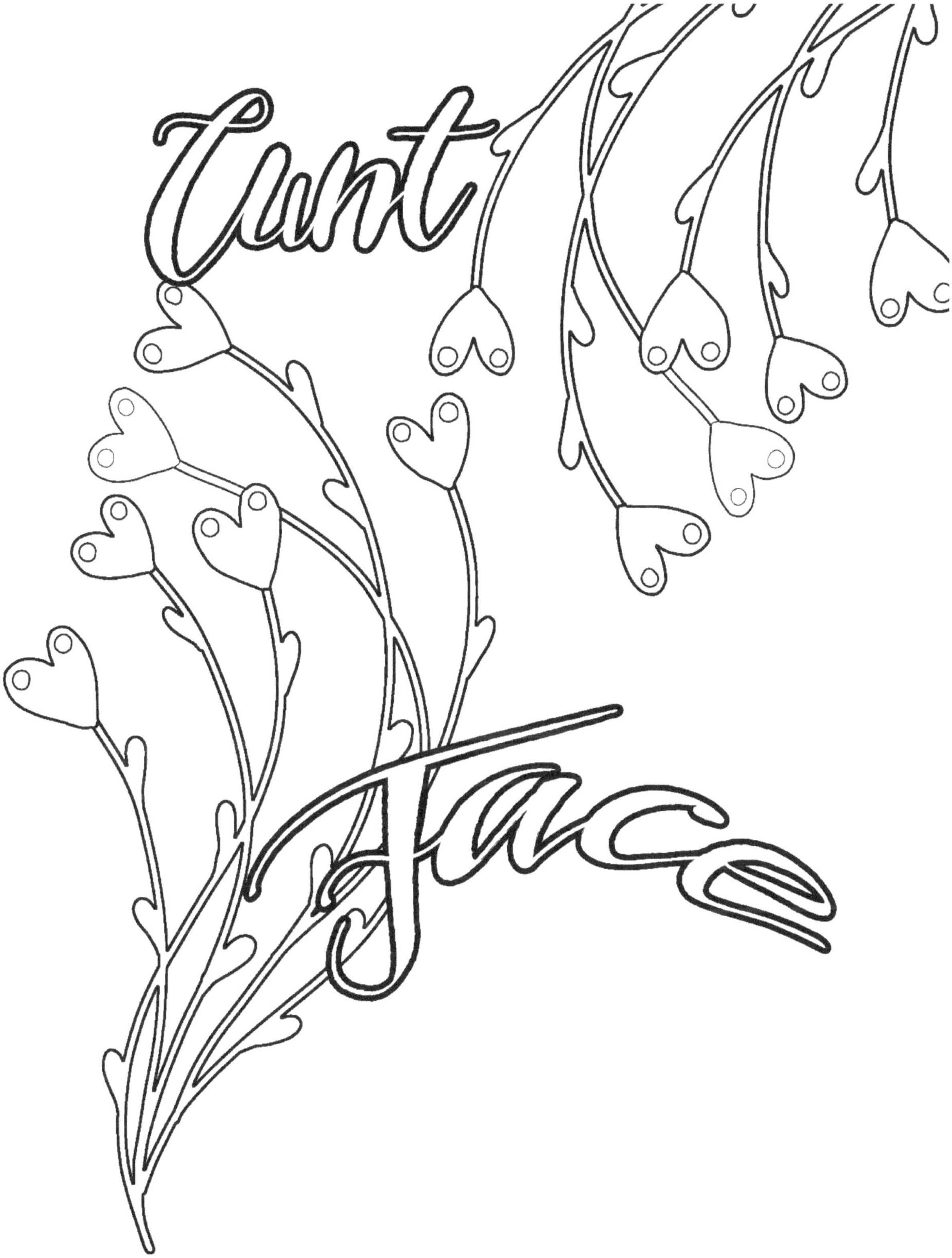
Cunt
face

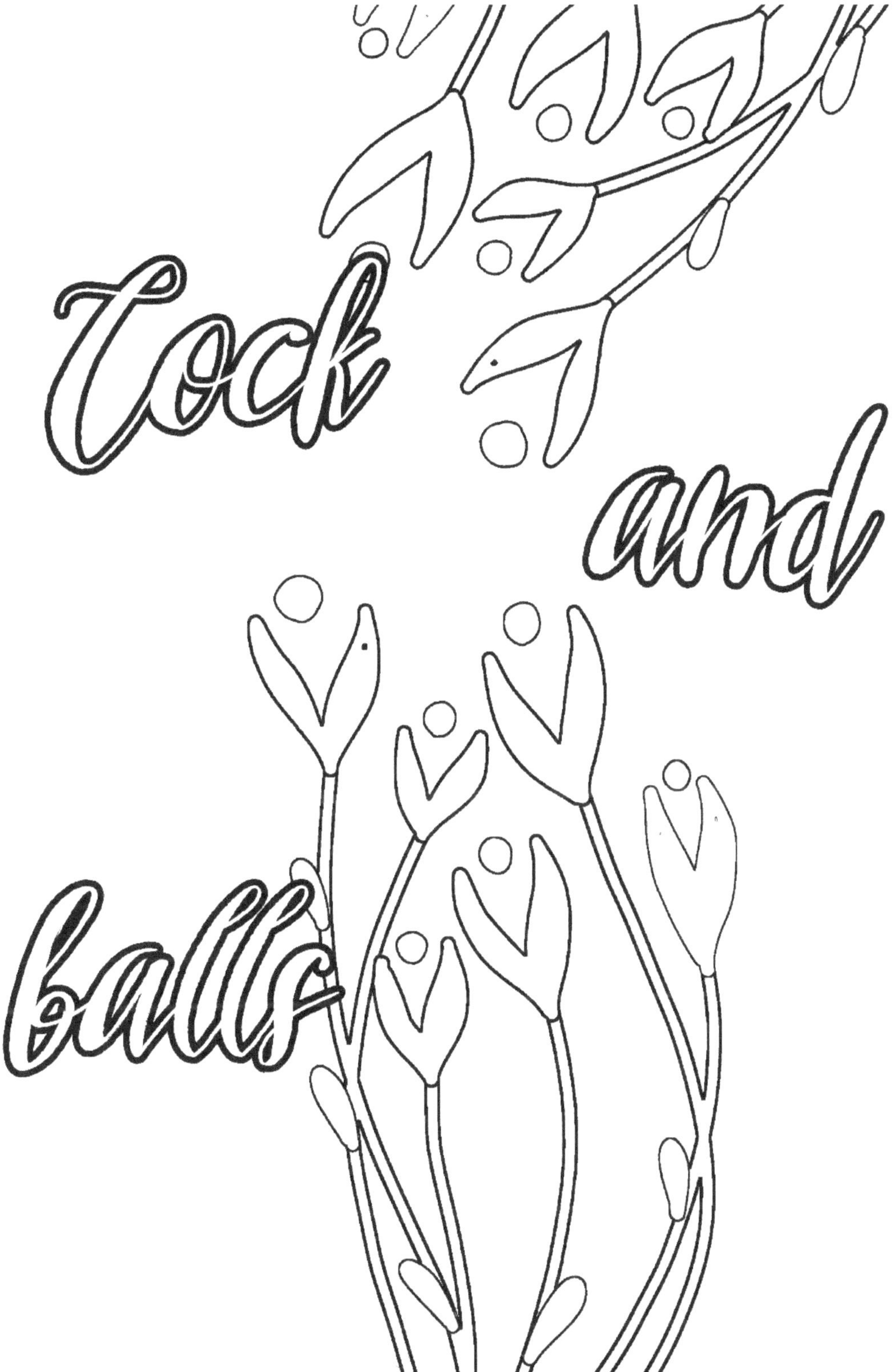
Cock
and
balls

Bastard

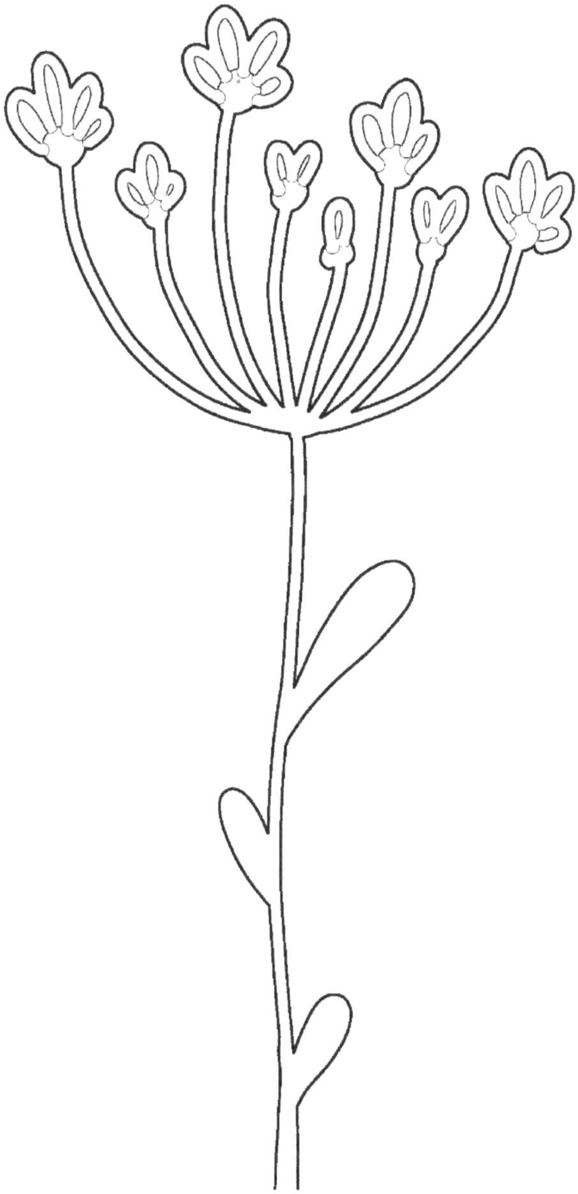

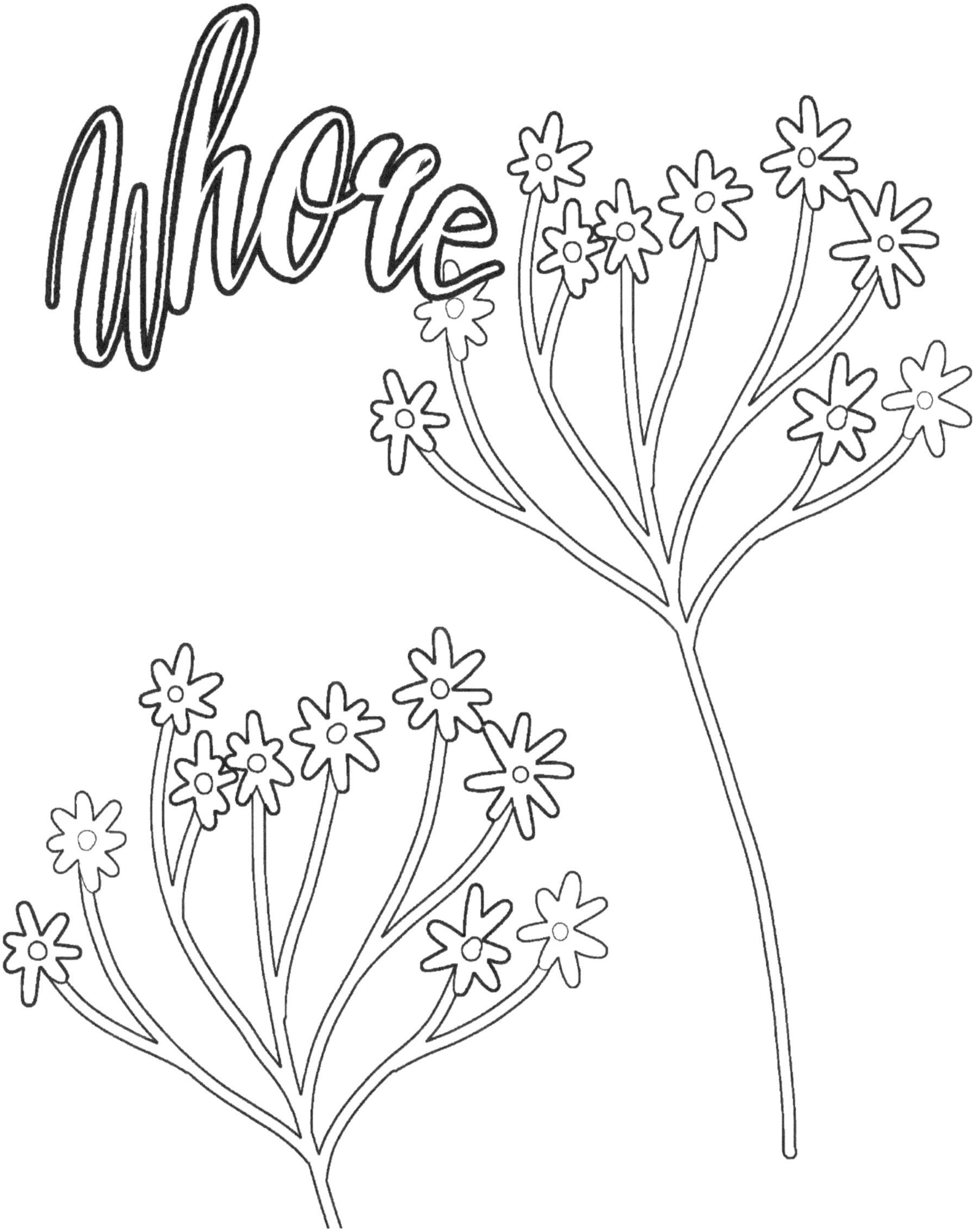
whore

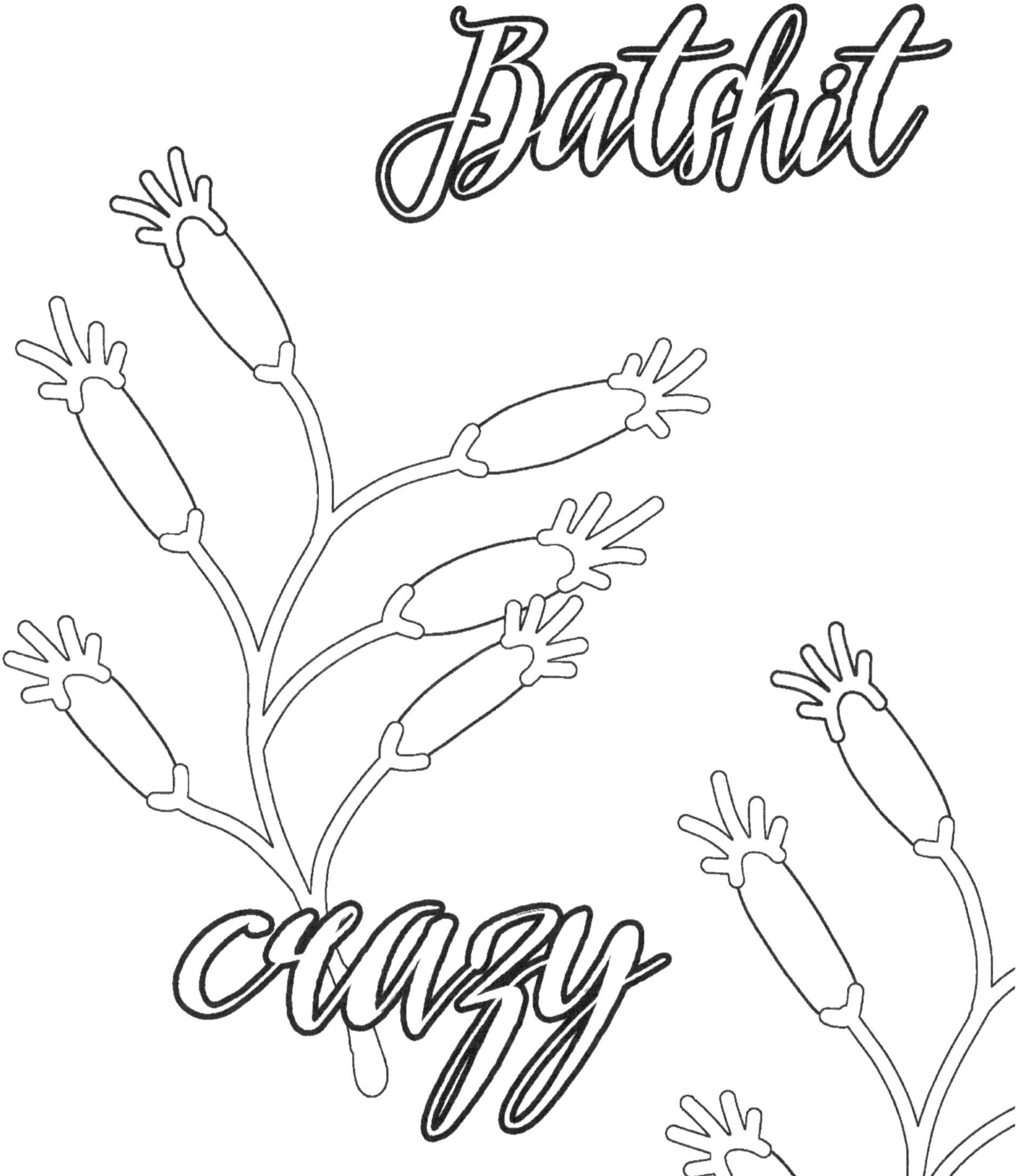
Batshit
crazy

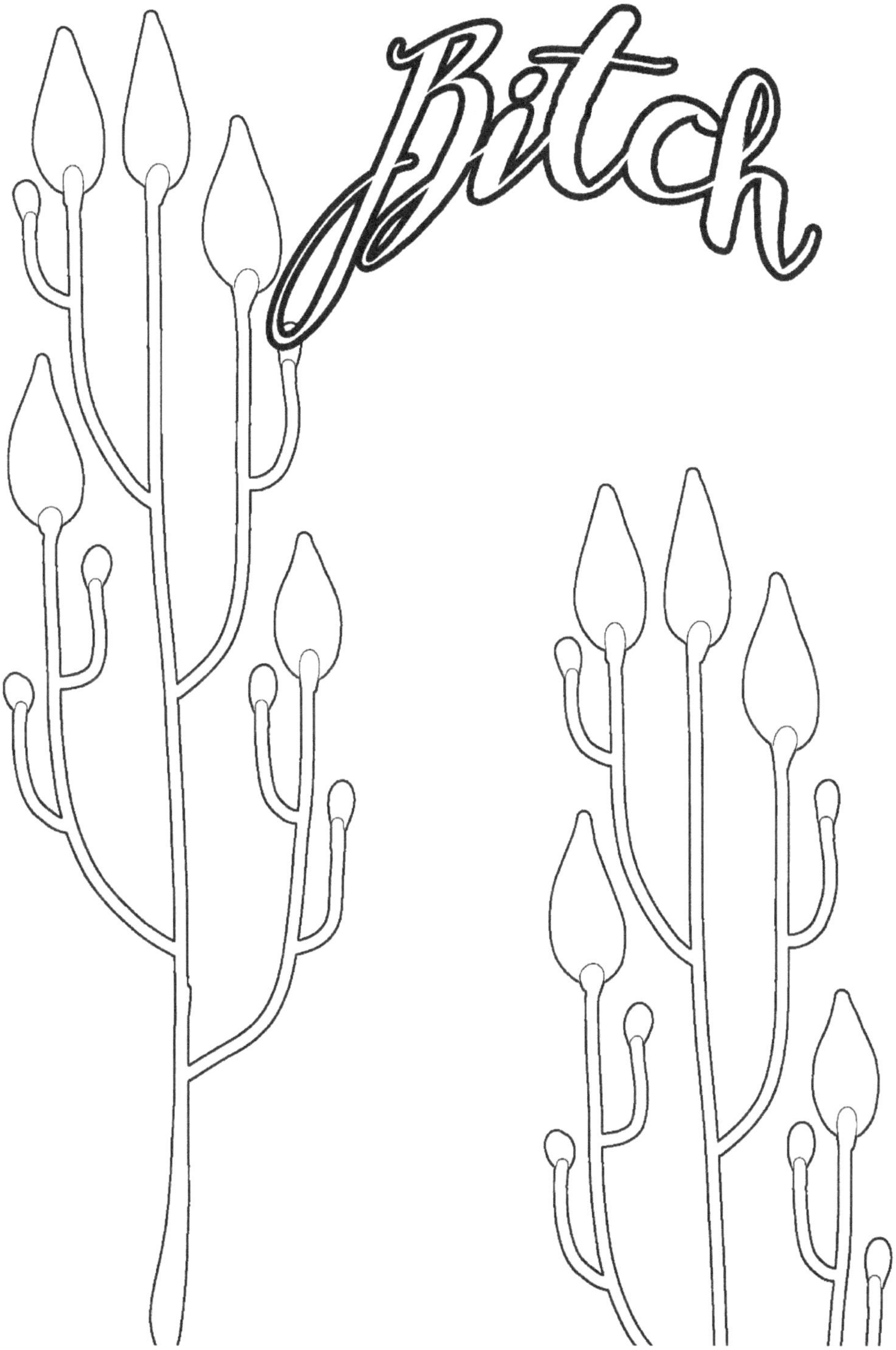
Bitch

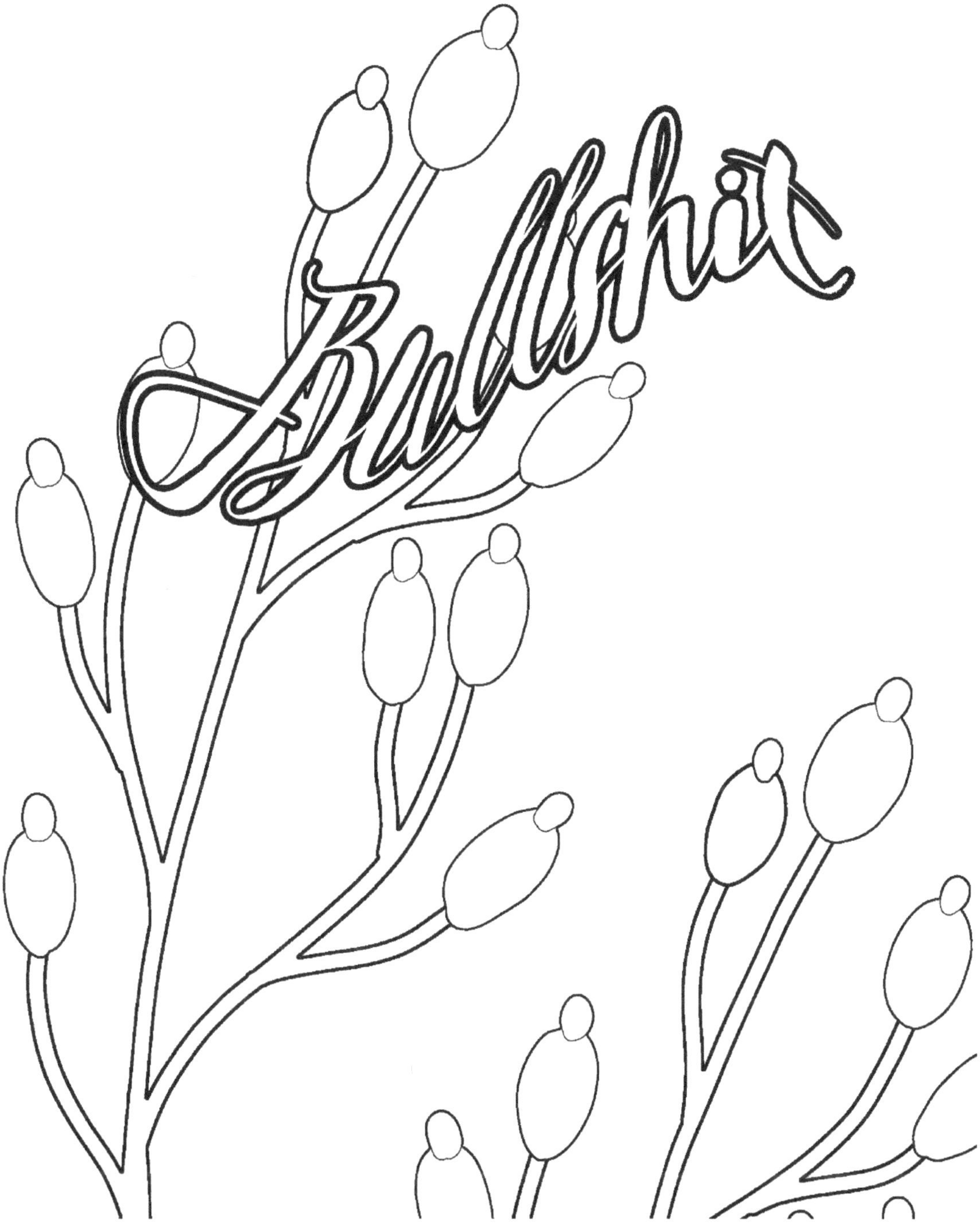
Bullshit

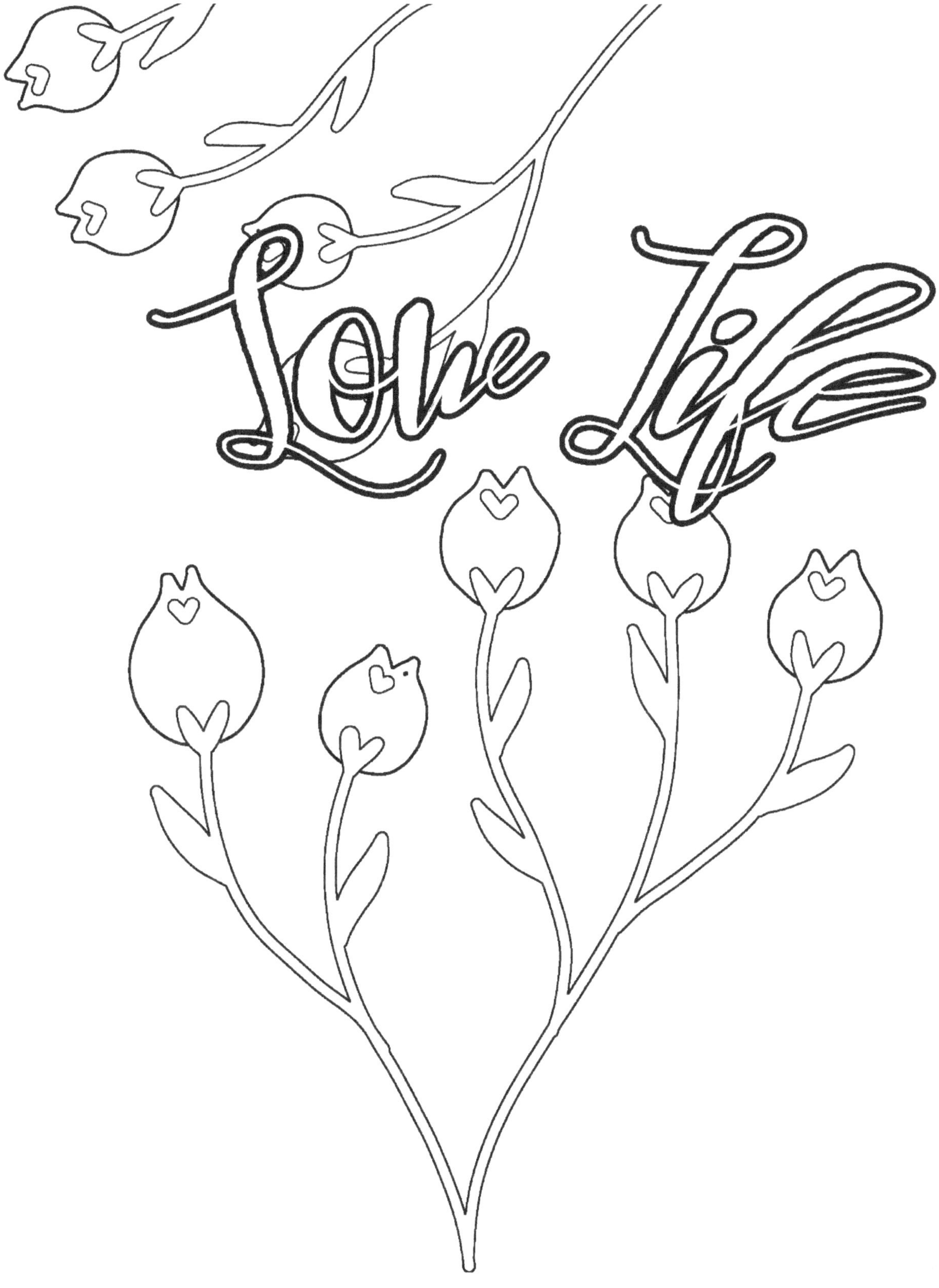
Love Life

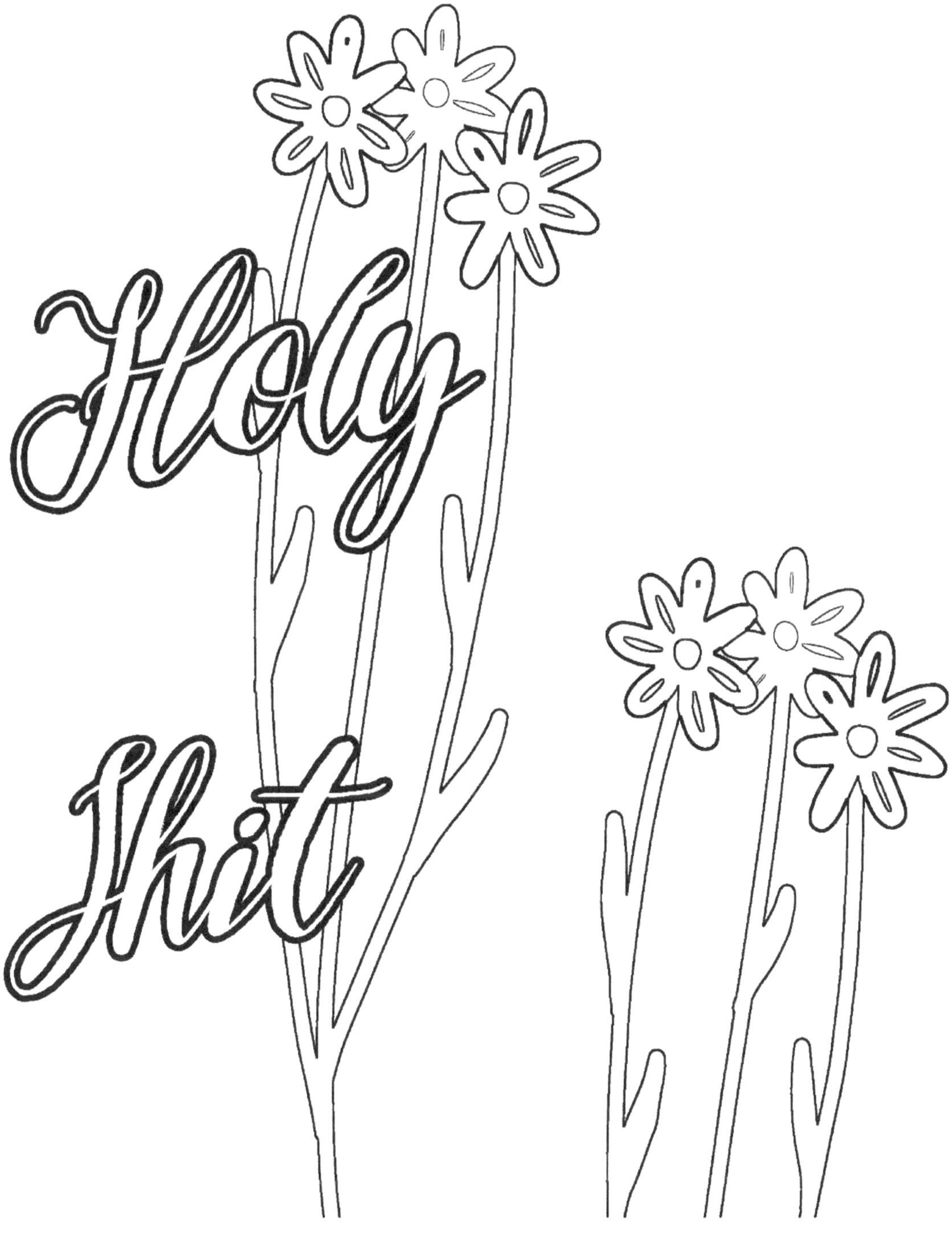
Holy
Shit

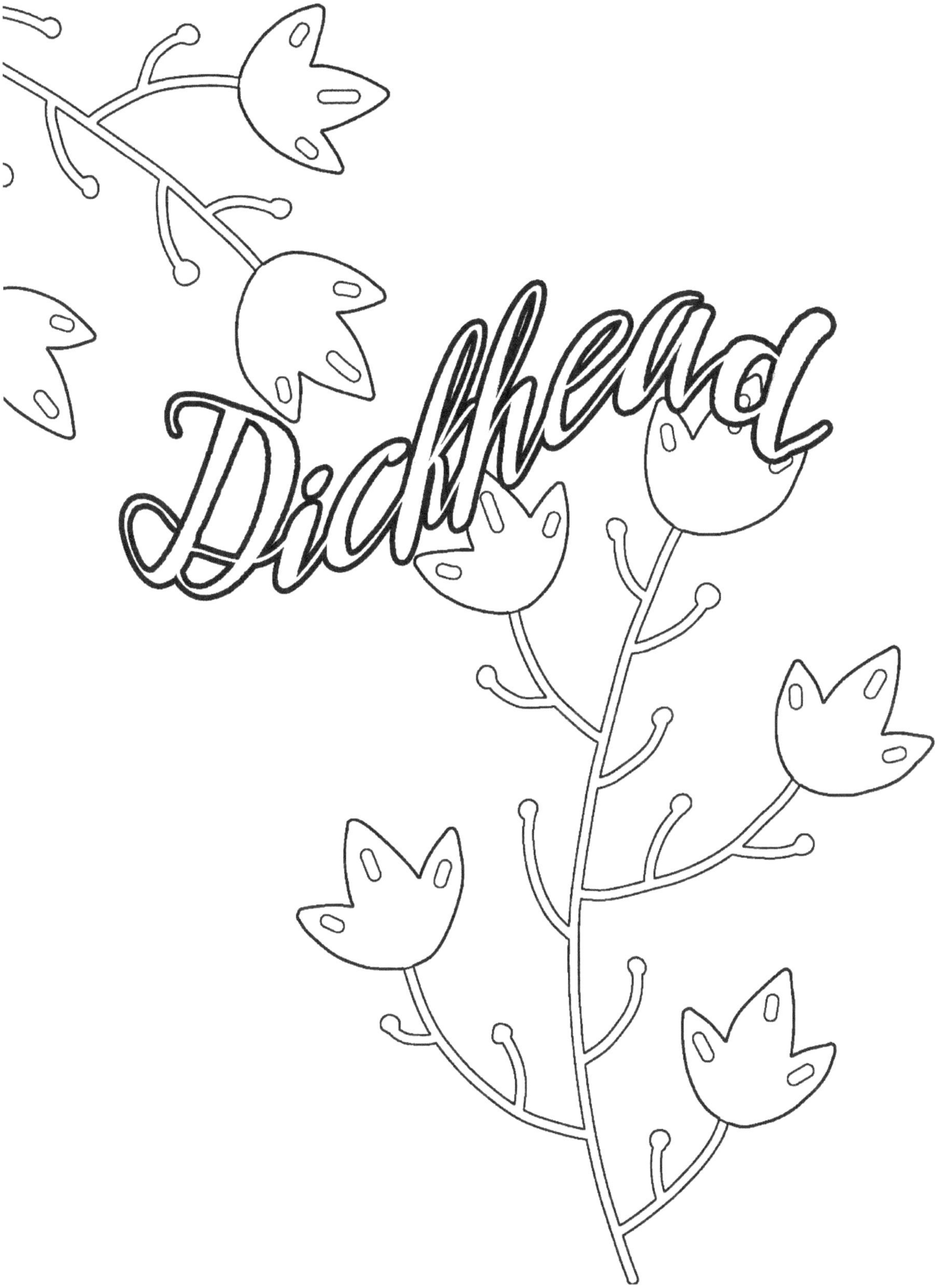
Dickhead

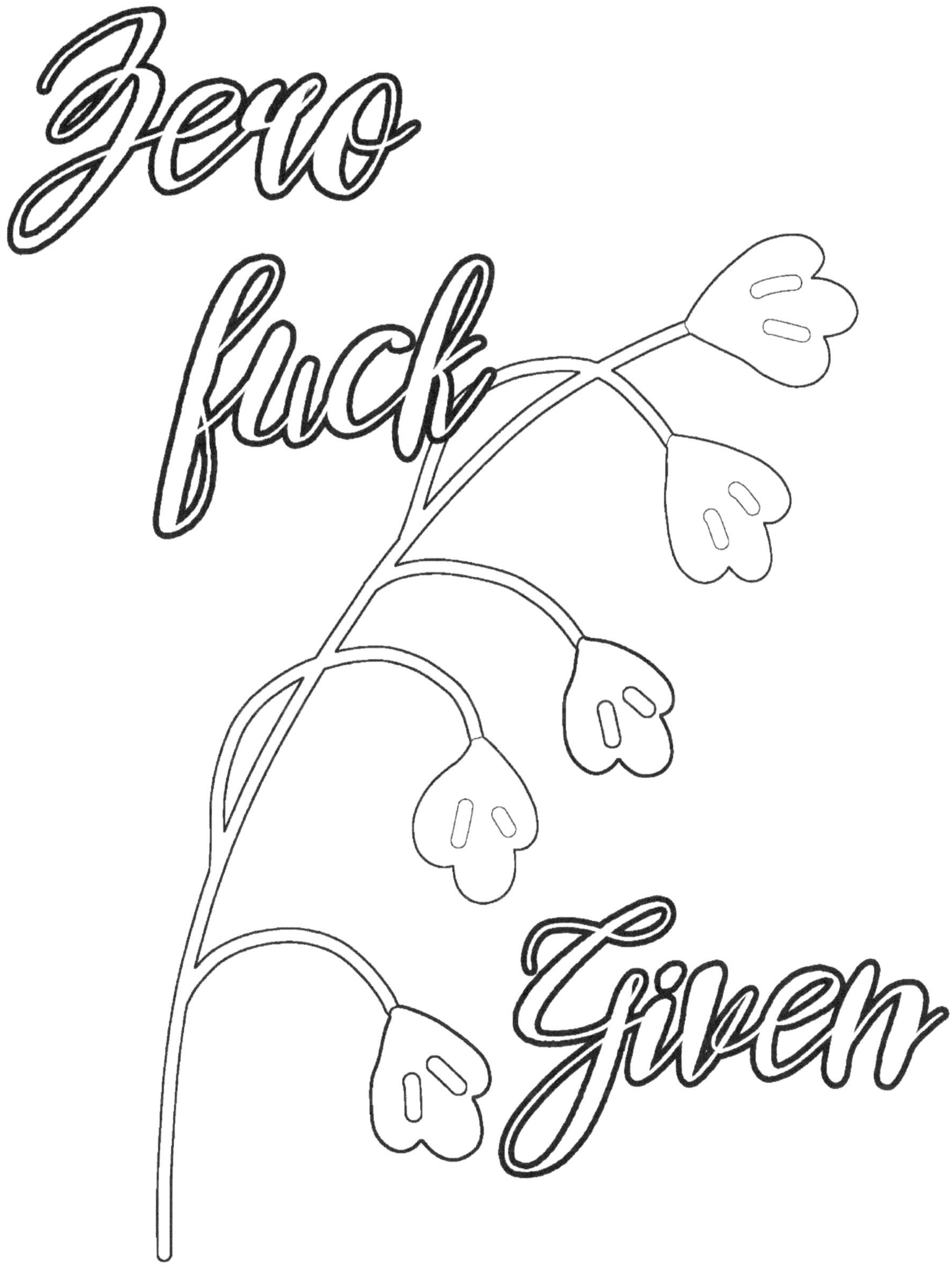
Zero
fuck
Given

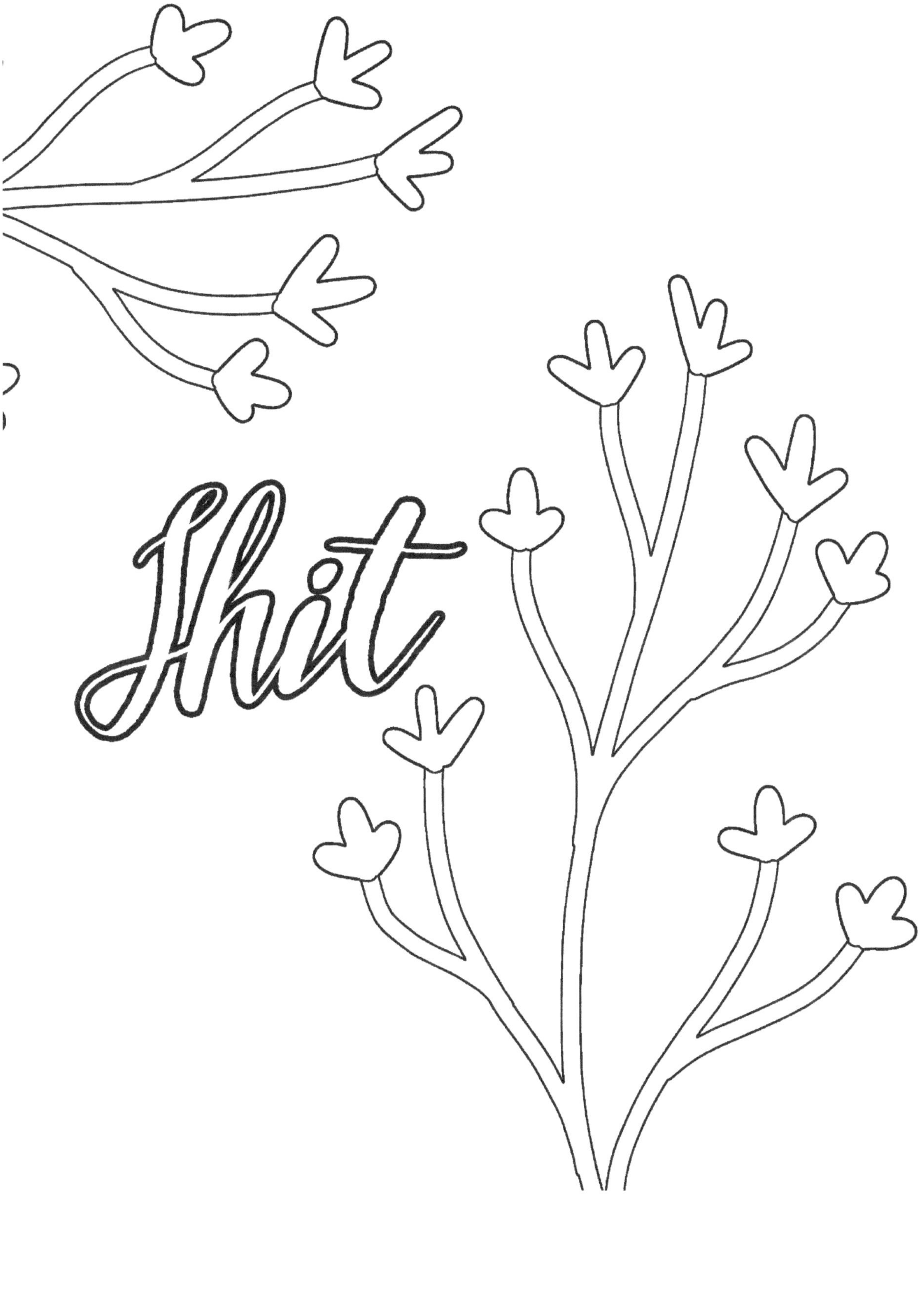
Shit

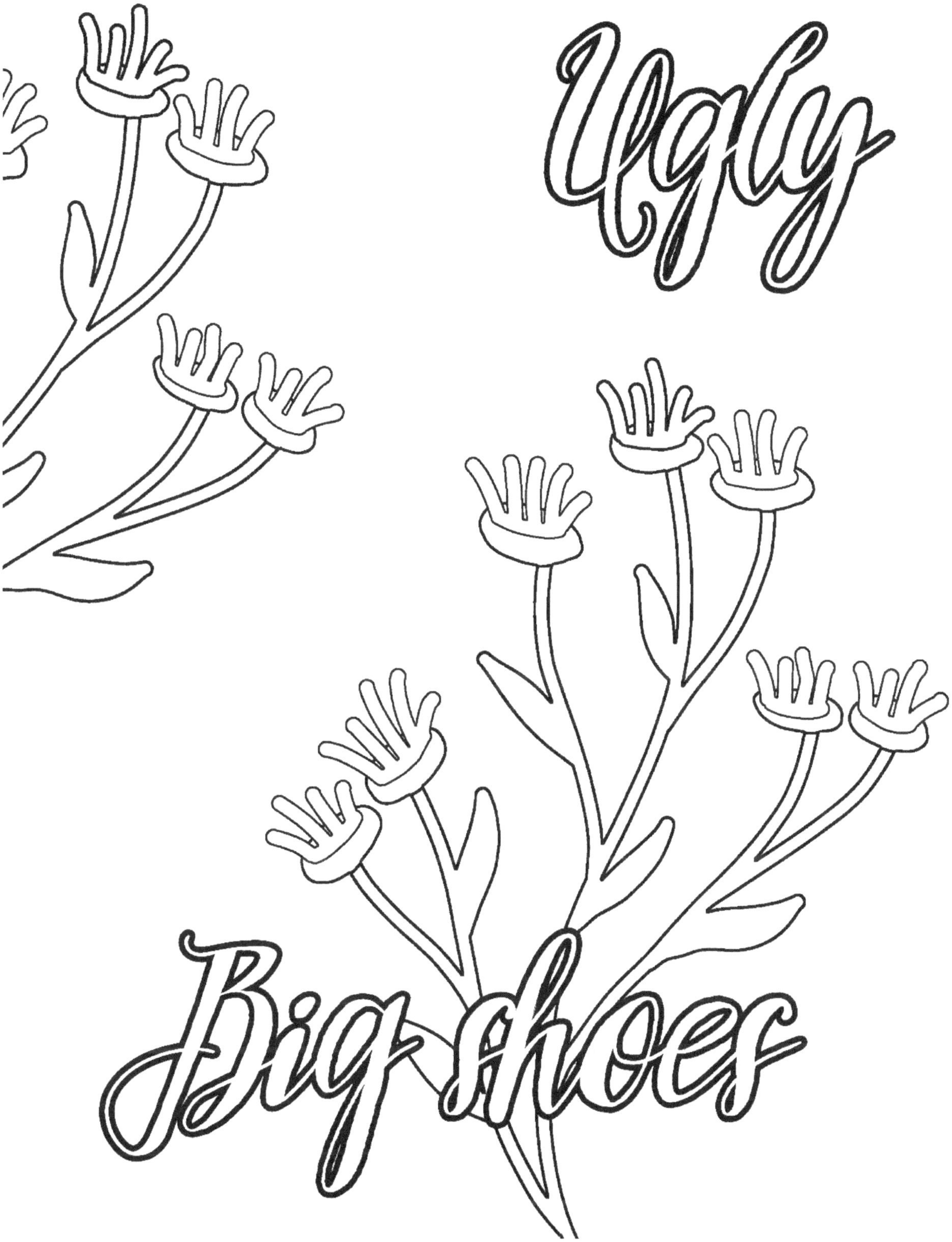
Ugly
Big shoes

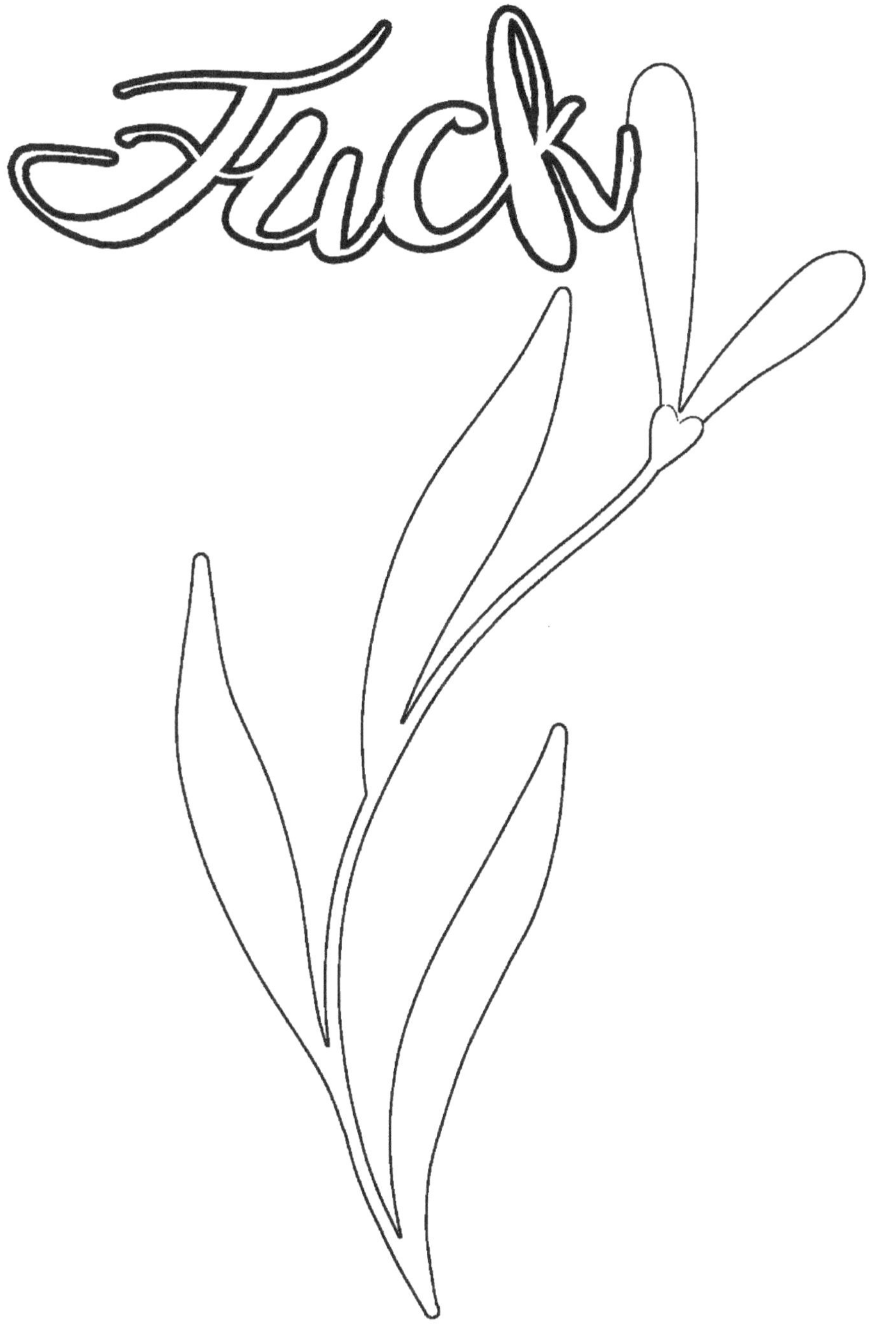
Fuck

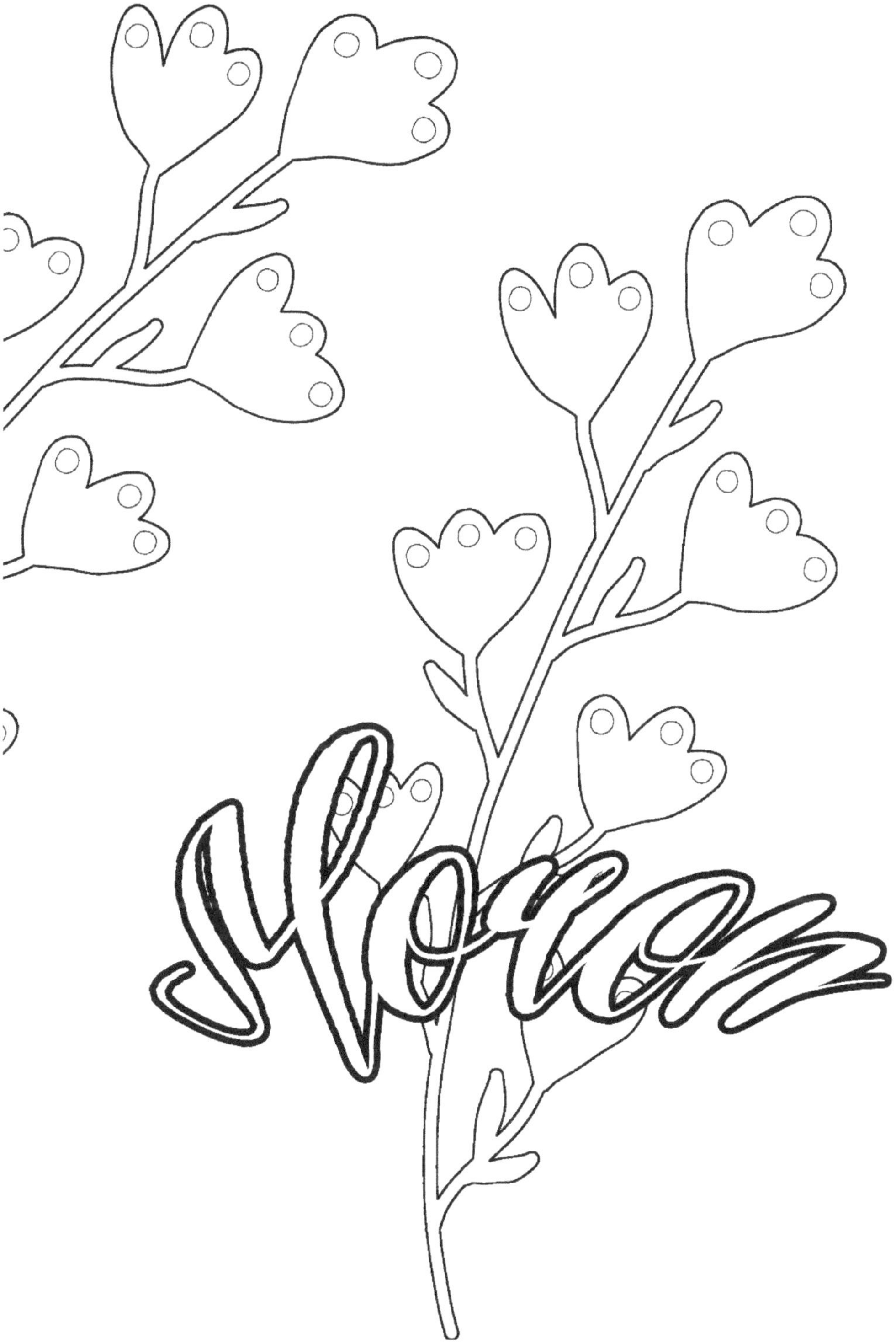

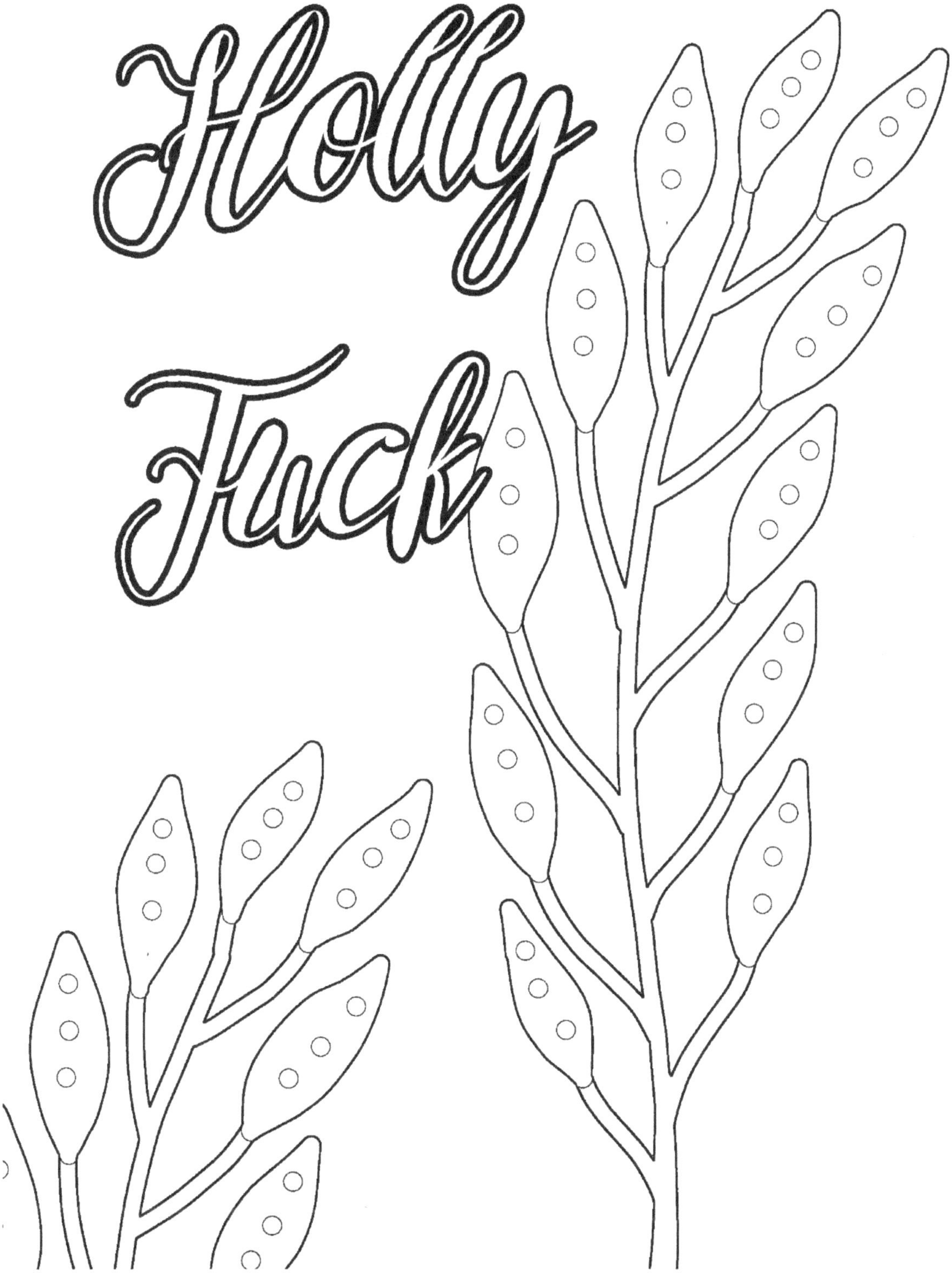
Holly
Fuck

Piss off

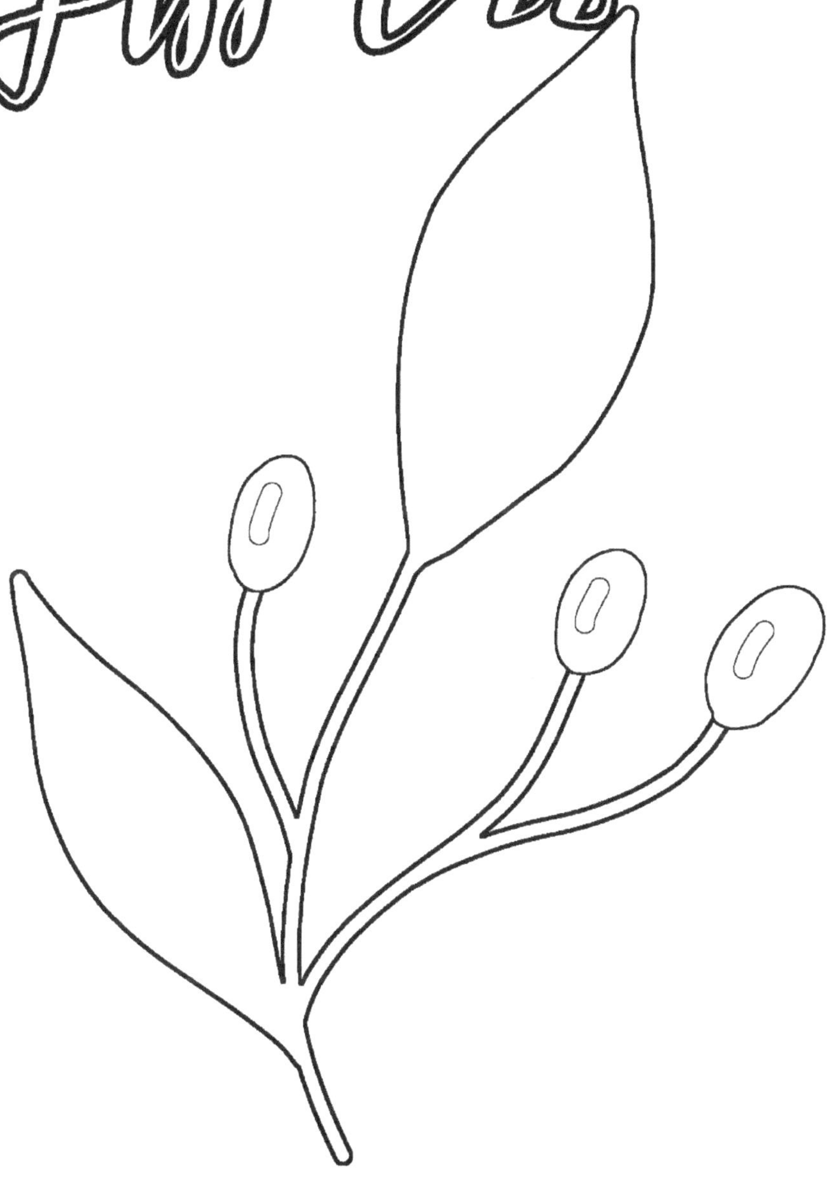

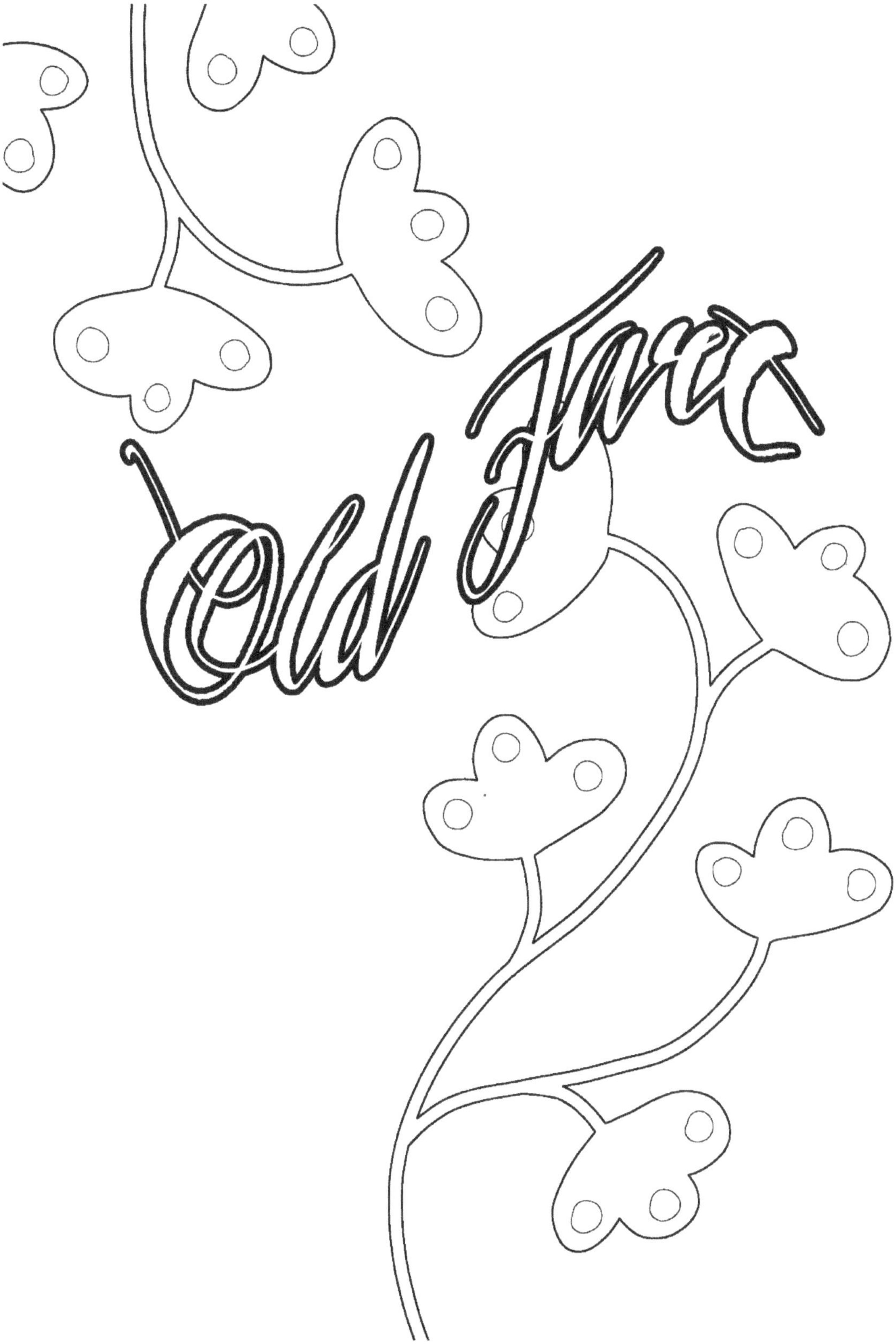
Old Fart

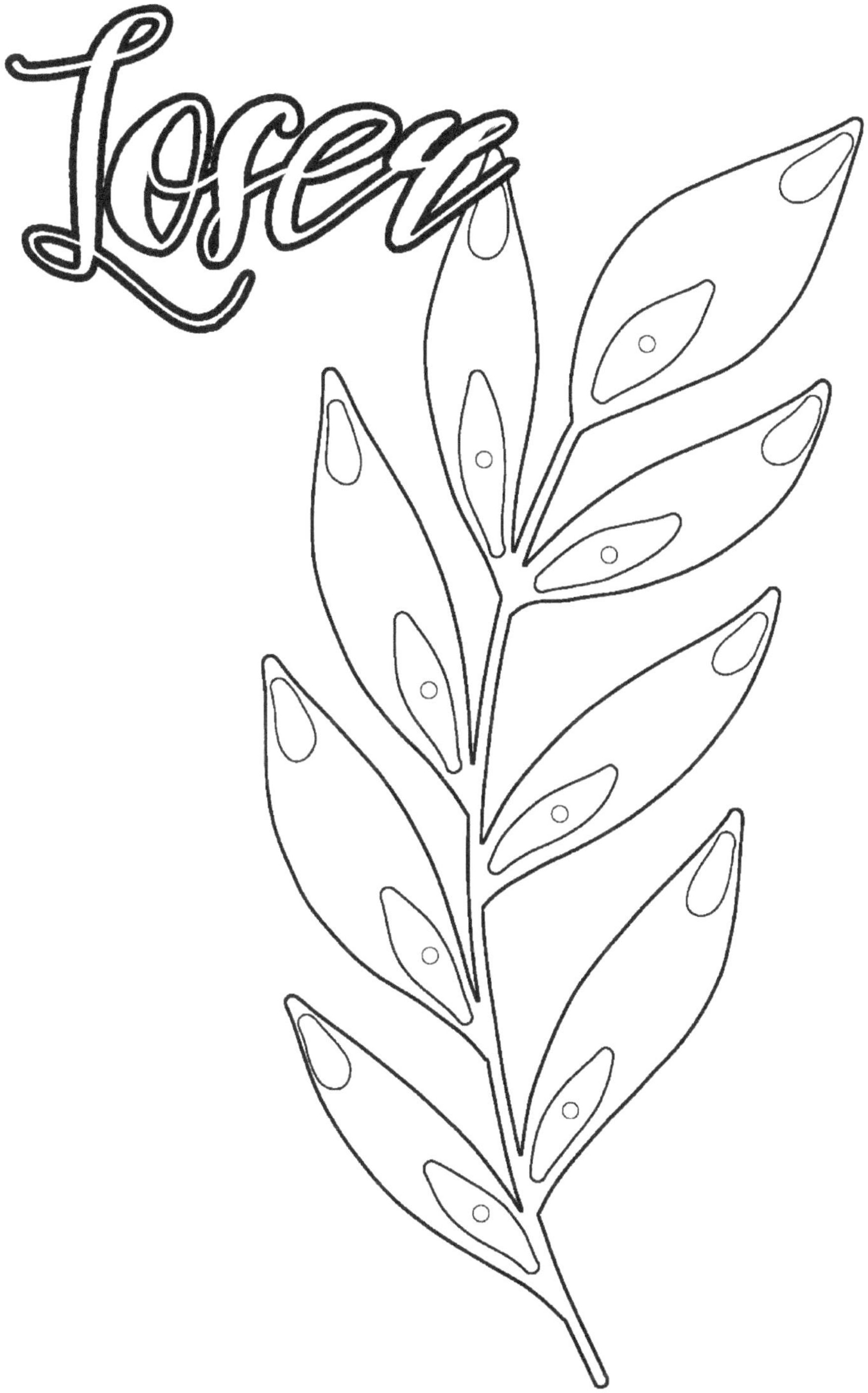
Loser

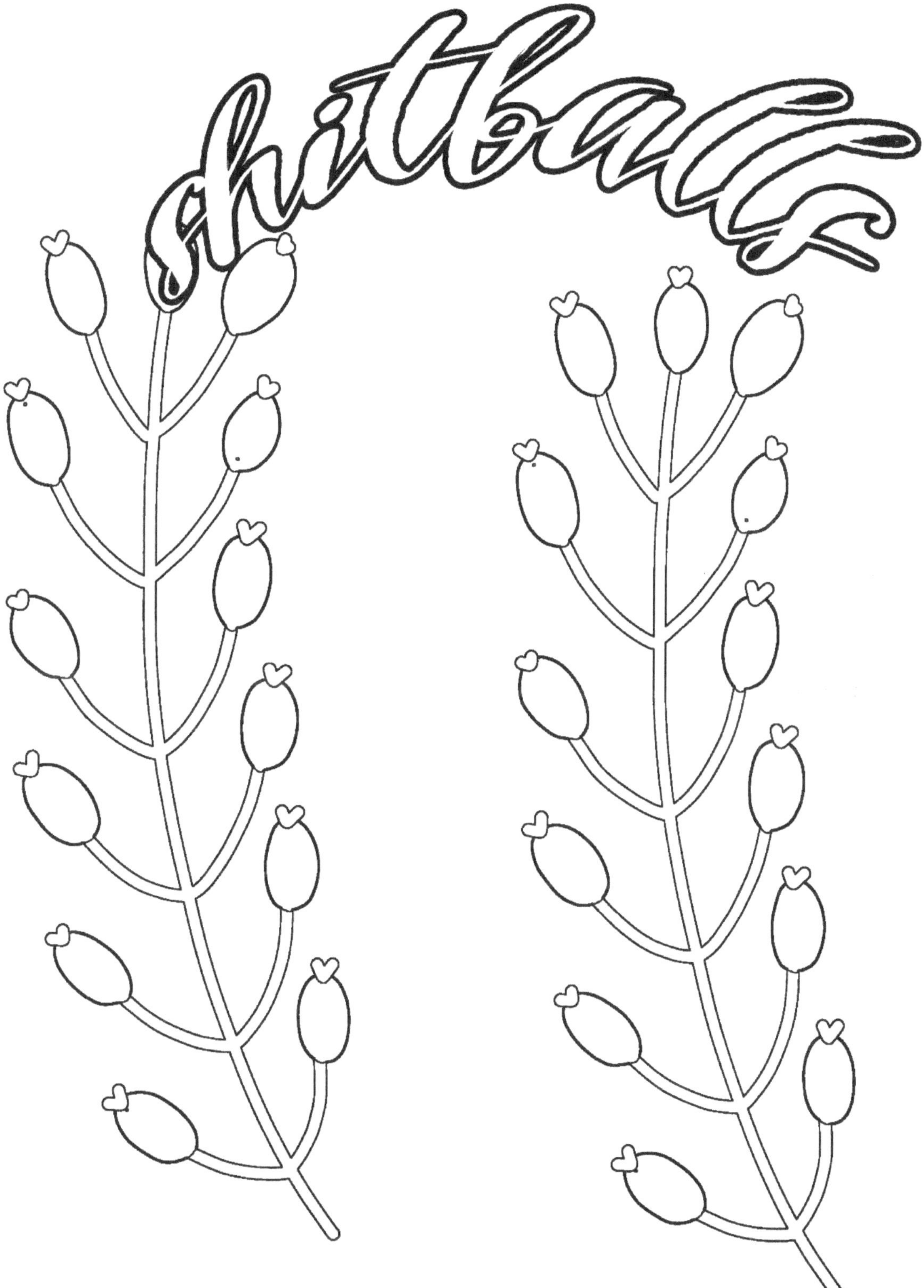
shitballs

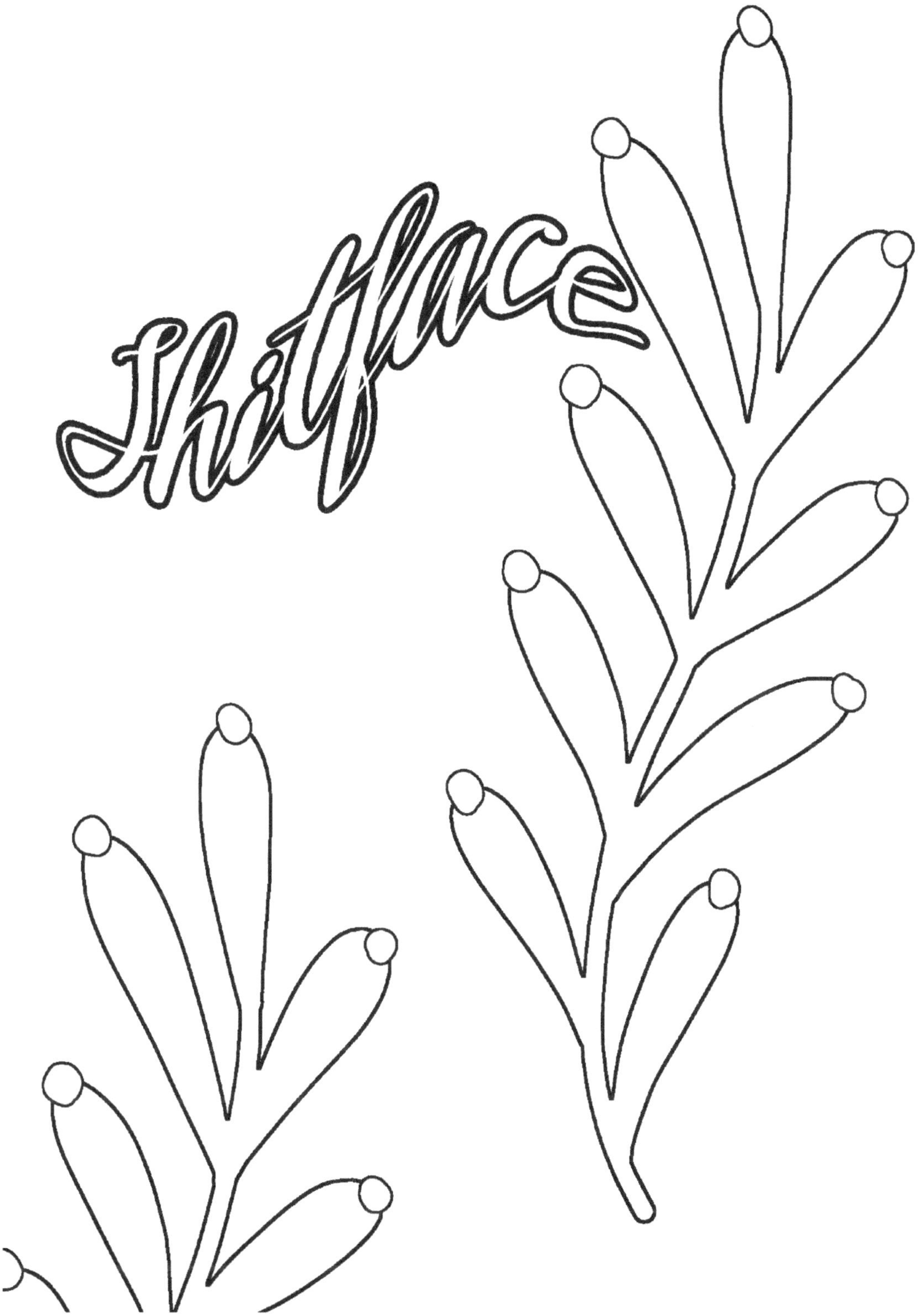
Shitface

HAVE A GOOD DAY.

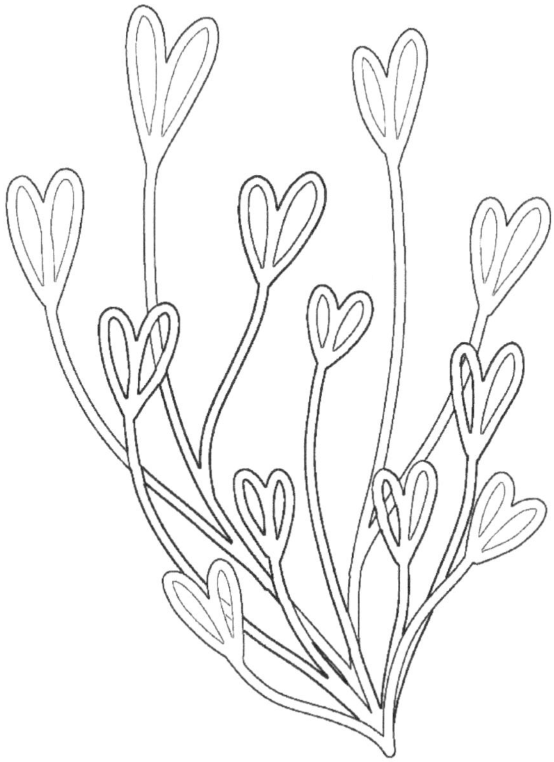

Note